Also by Gary Zukav

The Dancing Wu Li Masters:
An Overview of the New Physics

* *The Seat of the Soul*

* *Soul Stories*

Thoughts from the Seat of the Soul:
Meditations for Souls in Process

Also by Gary Zukav and Linda Francis

* *The Heart of the Soul:*
Emotional Awareness

THOUGHTS FROM THE

HEART
OF THE
SOUL

Meditations for Emotional Awareness

GARY ZUKAV
and
LINDA FRANCIS

A FIRESIDE BOOK
Published by Simon & Schuster

NEW YORK   LONDON   TORONTO   SYDNEY   SINGAPORE

FIRESIDE
Rockefeller Center
1230 Avenue of the Americas
New York, NY 10020

Second Fireside Edition 2001

FIRESIDE and colophon are registered trademarks
of Simon & Schuster, Inc.

For information about special discounts for bulk purchases,
please contact Simon & Schuster Special Sales:
1-800-456-6798 or business@simonandschuster.com

Designed by Joy O'Meara Battista

Manufactured in the United States of America

1   3   5   7   9   10   8   6   4   2

Library of Congress Cataloging-in-Publication Data is available.

ISBN 0-7432-3728-5

This book is dedicated to our
three beautiful granddaughters,
Jamie, Sydney, and Cady, and all the
grandchildren in the world.

"... learning how to look
inside ourselves ..."

FOREWORD

We hope this book will be helpful to you in learning how to use your emotions to assist you in your spiritual growth. Emotions are the force field of your soul. You cannot experience your soul without experiencing your emotions. In order to experience your emotions you must develop necessary skills. That is what this small book helps you to do. It provides you with thoughts—meditations—to remind you, guide you, nurture you, and support you in developing those skills.

These meditations come from the book *The Heart of the Soul: Emotional Awareness*. If you have read *The Heart of the Soul*, you may enjoy having some thoughts from it available to you in this convenient format. It is easy to read yet takes little space in your purse or pack. If thoughts that you encounter here are helpful to you, you can explore them in detail in *The Heart of the Soul*.

Emotional awareness is an important part of creating authentic power—the alignment of your personality with your soul. If you want to learn more about authentic power, you can read *The Seat of the Soul* or *Soul Stories*. You can also contact Genesis: The Foundation for the Universal Human, whose mission is to assist individuals in the creation of authentic power, at P.O. Box 339, Ashland, OR 97520, USA, and visit *www.universalhuman.org* or *www.zukav.com*.

We are honored to be a part of your journey.

Love,
Gary and Linda

The longest journey you will make is from your head to your heart. We are all on this journey.

Being aware of your emotions means being aware of pain. The only alternative is to mask it.

When you act with an empowered heart, you are free from compulsions, fixations, obsessions, and addictions.

Billions of humans live in poverty and suffer hunger, oppression, and brutality. Changing these circumstances requires the heart.

Spiritual growth is replacing survival as the central objective of the human experience.

Since our origin as a species, the need to feel safe, valuable, and loved has focused our attention outward. Now we are learning to look inside to find the roots of our insecurities, and to pull them out.

A new human species is being born that looks at the external world of things, interactions, and experiences as a mirror that reflects an internal world of intentions, emotions, and thoughts.

uthentic power is the alignment of your personality with your soul. It is being fully engaged in the present moment. You cannot align your personality with your soul without becoming conscious of your emotions.

The creation of authentic power confronts you with the unhealthiest parts of yourself—the parts that blame, criticize, judge, resent, envy, and hate others, yourself, and the Universe. These are the parts that must be acknowledged in order to change them.

An authentically empowered personality is so powerful that the idea of showing power through force is not even part of his or her consciousness.

We are all continually processing energy that flows through us. We experience those processes as emotions.

Energy continually flows into the top of your head, moves downward through your torso, and then returns to where it came from. The energy that flows through you is always pure and wholesome.

Y ou cannot grow spiritually without learning how to detach from your emotions and understand them as products of the way energy is processed in your own unique energy processing system.

Each emotion is a signal from your soul. When you ignore or repress emotions, you lose important information.

Your emotions are your best friends because they do not leave you. They bring to your attention what you need to know.

Your emotional landscape is as unique as your body, your aptitudes, and your interests.

Emotions are classes in the Earth school. Some classes are about fear, and some are about love. The Universe is your tutor, and your classroom is your life. The main course in the Earth school, Authentic Power, is the same for everyone, but different students need different courses in order to complete it.

You cannot change all of the people that make you angry, sad, or jealous, but you can change yourself. You begin that process by looking inward.

No matter where or how energy leaves your system, it produces an emotion.

E nergy leaves you in fear and doubt,
or in love and trust.

Painful emotions are flags that call your attention to what you need to change in yourself.

Every emotion is a physical experience. Recognizing how and where energy leaves your energy processing system is the foundation of spiritual growth.

When energy leaves the processing location in your chest in love and trust, you are open and connected to all Life. When energy leaves it in fear and doubt, your chest hurts. "Heartache" is more than an emotional state—it is a physical condition.

Emotional pain of any kind is a reminder to stop and look inside.

Physical pain in the vicinity of your solar plexus is produced by fears that you cannot provide for yourself, defend yourself, or do what you need to do. When energy leaves the processing center near the solar plexus in fear and doubt, you feel it "in the pit of your stomach."

Painful sensations in your chest are produced when you fear that you cannot love or be loved.

When you fear you cannot express yourself, or that you will not be heard if you do, you feel a constriction in your throat, or you have a hoarse or weak voice, or your neck or shoulders become tight.

The energy center at the base of the torso connects you with the Earth. When energy leaves this center in love and trust, you feel at home on the Earth.

As you come to understand your energy processing system and how it works, you can understand your emotions, even those that are difficult to deal with.

Think of your emotions as presents, waiting to be unwrapped. Unwrapping is an important part of your spiritual journey.

Energy leaving your energy processing system in fear and doubt causes painful sensations.

Feeling your emotions is a physical experience.

S piritual growth requires you to become aware of everything you are
feeling, all the time.

Medical treatment is emergency care for symptoms that have developed over a long period of time. The symptom is the flower on a plant. Treating the symptom is picking the flower, while the plant remains untouched.

Emotional awareness is preventive medicine because physical dysfunction results when you release energy in fear and doubt for years.

Releasing energy in love and trust produces health and vitality.

We are all souls temporarily utilizing our bodies, which are our vehicles for the journey. The engine of the vehicle is the energy processing system. Emotions are the instruments that tell us how the engine is functioning.

S canning your energy processing system at each location, moment to moment, is emotional awareness. Ignoring this information will eventually cause your vehicle to break down. No illness is sudden.

The more distressing the emotion, the more painful are the sensations in your body, and the more compulsive are your thoughts.

If you think you are a person who feels nothing, or very little, think again. Everyone feels physical pain. If pain is continually present, it begins to feel normal.

The difference between not feeling pain and believing that you do not feel pain is the difference between being able to enjoy yourself, create freely, and live without fear, or not.

People who think they feel nothing are especially bound by the fears they think they don't have.

If you feel nothing, know that painful sensations are there whether you feel them or not. Keep looking. If you don't make this effort, the sensations will eventually break down the barriers you've constructed.

You cannot create a life of fulfillment, joy, and meaning while you are barricading yourself from others and from the opportunities Life offers you.

Walking through your emotional landscape without paying attention to what's there is like walking through a meadow without paying attention to what's growing.

Before you become aware of your emotional landscape, all you can see are the intense emotions that grip your attention now and then.

The more familiar you become with your emotions, the more easily you will be able to see how they remain the same, even though the circumstances in which they appear change. The circumstances that trigger your anger, for example, may change, but your anger does not.

Energy leaves your energy processing system in ways that are specific to you. As you practice putting your sensations and thoughts together, you will recognize repeating combinations, enabling you to connect the dots and plot the map of your emotional landscape.

You are always in the present moment. If you are not aware of this, you have no power because you are under the control of external circumstances.

When you are aware of the present moment, you have access to all possibilities that the present moment offers.

It is not possible to become aware of the present moment by examining, studying, or thinking about external circumstances. The more you become absorbed in these activities, the less aware of the present moment you are.

Your inner landscape is the anchor of your experience. It is richer than your outer landscape, no matter how magnificent the sunrise, how awesome the night sky, or how immense the turbulent ocean that is rushing toward you.

Throughout your life, your inner landscape presents its contents to you again and again. When you are aware of all its elements, you are in continual communication with your soul.

Painful emotions, such as jealousy, anger, fear, and vengefulness, are indicators of the parts of your soul that your soul desires to heal.

Emotions that feel good, such as gratitude, contentment, and appreciation, are experiences of the parts of your soul that are already healthy.

The more painful the communication with your soul—the more painful the emotion—the more compulsive is the desire to avoid the communication. When the pain of the communication with your soul becomes intense, you are at a pivotal moment of decision.

Remaining with your inner experience is choosing to pursue authentic power.

E motional pain is physical pain.

D o not worry about what emotions you are feeling. Direct your attention to what your body feels.

Each thought is accompanied by emotions, but if you are not willing to examine what your body is experiencing in the moment, you will divert yourself into thoughts, plans, ideas, calculations, and judgments.

Intellectual endeavor and emotional awareness are not mutually exclusive, but when an intellectual pursuit becomes compulsive, it is used to divert attention from painful emotions.

C ompulsion is the unfolding of
fear.

The first step in uncovering the origin of a compulsion is the hardest. You must stop doing what is compulsive and experience what you feel when you do.

As long as you do not know what you are experiencing inside, you are asleep in your life, even though you may think that you are very much awake.

Emotional awareness is the healing remedy for a fixation on external circumstances.

Passion is the unfolding of joy.

Awareness of the present moment requires detachment from both your outer landscape and your inner landscape.

D etachment allows you to remain aware of what you feel while the events of your life unfold.

When you are not detached from your emotions, you cannot separate yourself from them, and they possess you.

When you are aware of your emotions, you are in a position to change how energy is moving through you. You step into the present moment.

Intimacy is natural for us. We are designed to be caring, sensitive, and loving toward one another.

Intimacy requires vulnerability.

Intimacy and the pursuit of external power—the ability to manipulate and control—are incompatible.

The experience of intimacy is not related to how others act or do not act, or how they speak or do not speak. It is dependent upon how energy leaves your energy processing system.

When you naturally create harmony, cooperation, sharing, and reverence for Life, you cannot suffer from lack of intimacy.

When you do not recognize your deeper, painful emotions for what they are, these emotions shape your perceptions, judgments, and actions. They become a wall between you and others as real as a wall made of concrete and steel.

Anger is an attempt to change others in ways that make you feel more secure.

The more frightened you are, the more righteous you become, and the more others appear to be at fault.

All painful emotions are expressions of fear.

Intimacy comes from trusting the Universe to provide what you need, when you need it, and in the manner that is the most appropriate for you.

Intimacy is letting your guard down. You welcome the world instead of resisting it.

GARY ZUKAV AND LINDA FRANCIS

Intimacy allows every circumstance to become a gift.

You reshape the world by reshaping yourself. The question is not how to change others, but how to change yourself.

When you awake as a student in the Earth school, all that you encounter is your teacher.

You create intimacy when you shift from the pursuit of external power—the ability to manipulate and control—to the pursuit of authentic power, the alignment of your personality with your soul.

Most people use their energy attempting to rearrange circumstances that trigger painful emotions. Changing external circumstances will not change your rigid patterns of emotional response. That requires looking at the patterns themselves.

Your patterns of emotional response have a life that is independent of particular external circumstances.

You encounter circumstances that trigger painful emotions until you look beyond them to the interior dynamics that create your emotional pain. When you do this, you are on the journey that you were born to take.

Anger is an iceberg phenomenon. Beneath every experience of anger is a huge body of emotional experience.

nger lashes out at a target and assumes the role of judge, jury, and executioner. There is no appeal.

Individuals who become angry think they are familiar with their emotions because of their outbursts. They are not. Angry outbursts are painful experiences, but they are not emotional explorations.

All hostility originates in fear.

Love is fearless.

Anger is the agony of believing that you are not capable of being understood, and that you are not worthy of being understood.

An angry individual appears not to be frightened. Actually, he or she is terrified. Beneath anger is pain, and beneath pain is fear.

When you become angry, you bury pain. The angrier you become, the more you push it away.

An individual who is continually angry is in continual pain. Your anger is your resistance to feeling the pain.

The core cause of anger is a lack of self-worth. Rage is an excruciating experience of powerlessness.

When you are consumed by uncontrollable anger, you are diverting all of your energy into avoiding your emotions.

L ife is a journey into vulnerability, and when you are angry, you do not trust. When you feel worthless, you are terrified by your life.

The Universe provides you with opportunities, again and again, without cessation, to move into the fullness of your power—into the unobstructed perception of your worth, your value, and your responsibilities.

Detachment is the difference between emotional involvement and emotional awareness. Detachment allows you to see your emotions as they form, develop, intensify, and change.

Emotional involvement is not the same as emotional awareness.

Emotional awareness is the ability to see the larger dynamic beneath the surface. Emotional involvement allows you to see only a small part of that dynamic, like the tip of an iceberg.

Most people go through their lives from one iceberg strike to another, from one experience of rage or jealousy or resentment to another. Workaholism is a way to steam full speed ahead without even posting a lookout.

Workaholism is a flight from emotions.

Workaholism is a drug as effective as a powerful anesthetic. Like all anesthetics, it wears off, and the pain returns.

Workaholism is magnetically attractive because it prevents the experience of any emotions.

Workaholism is the exploitation of people and circumstances in order to avoid pain.

When you indulge in workaholism, you put strangers in charge of your life while you focus obsessively on your job, a career, a remodeling project. The strangers are your emotions.

When your awareness is focused only on accomplishment, you experience only the temporary satisfaction that comes with completing a project. That is quickly replaced by the need to accomplish something else.

Workaholism is a deep sleep that prevents you from stepping into the power and purpose of your life.

When you feel angry, stop what you are doing, saying, and thinking. Focus your attention on what you are feeling.

Choosing not to act on an angry impulse and to feel the pain that lies beneath it is a very courageous thing to do.

Most people do things we think of as brave—such as driving racing cars or jumping out of airplanes—to avoid facing the pain they feel.

Anger hurts, but it is less painful than what causes it. Anger is a flight from feelings, like workaholism. That is why they go together.

E motional awareness allows you to walk the Earth awake instead of in a self-imposed trance.

Emotional awareness is continuously studying the changing array of emotions within you. It requires your attention.

Being tossed helplessly from emotion to emotion is a way of avoiding emotional exploration. There are numerous ways to avoid painful emotions, but none of them are effective indefinitely. All of them delay addressing the underlying causes of emotions.

Individuals who appear to be conversant with their emotions are not necessarily emotionally aware. Frequently they don't know the meaning of what they feel.

E motional literacy requires dedication and hard work.

Emotions that pass through you and are used to manipulate other people are like ripples on the surface of the ocean. They are not the same as currents that run deep.

In the pass-through effect, emotions are used to manipulate others. The one who feels the emotions and uses them to manipulate others remains unchanged.

People who are compulsively intellectual do not know what they are feeling.

D epression is a surface emotional
phenomenon, even though it is a
very painful experience. There is
much beneath it.

The experience of depression without the perspective that allows it to be used as an instrument of spiritual growth is the same as drifting on an ocean of pain in a vessel that is seaworthy and not taking the time to learn how to sail it.

Anger always accompanies depression.

Anger is the path of least resistance. Rage, emotional withdrawal, seething resentment, compulsive criticism, and the hunger for revenge all mask a pain so intense that it is unapproachable.

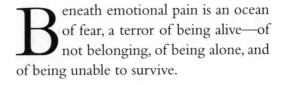

Beneath emotional pain is an ocean of fear, a terror of being alive—of not belonging, of being alone, and of being unable to survive.

Lack of self-worth is the fundamental source of all emotional pain. A feeling of insecurity, unworthiness, and lack of value is the core experience of powerlessness.

Reaching outward to fill inner holes is the pursuit of external power. The new evolutionary pathway of humankind is looking inward, finding the source of our insecurities, and healing them.

Emotions are signposts that point to parts of yourself that require healing. As you become aware of everything you are feeling all the time, you embark upon the path of spiritual growth.

Perfectionism is the assumption that the world is imperfect. This is incorrect. Every circumstance is perfect.

Perfectionism assumes that one choice is better than another, but all choices create perfect circumstances.

The choice that each individual makes is never between what is perfect and what is flawed; it is between perfection and perfection. Striving to avoid imperfection is useless.

W hat you prefer is not superior
to what others prefer.

The pursuit of external power—the ability to control and manipulate—is insisting that the circumstances that you prefer are perfect for others, too.

Judging your circumstances to be imperfect keeps you from seeing clearly the choices you have made, the choices that created your circumstances.

When you see clearly the relationship between the choices you've made and the circumstances around you, you will see the perfection of your circumstances. Then you will be able to change them.

Perfection is everywhere. It is your life and all that is in it. It is the compassion and wisdom that continually nudge you toward greater awareness and freedom.

Perfectionism is an intellectual exercise that draws attention away from your emotions and prevents the exploration of your creative power.

When you strive for perfection, you compare different versions of what could be instead of being present with what is. Perfectionism is an attempt to inhabit an imaginary world in order to avoid experiencing the world in which you live.

Experiencing the world in which you live requires your heart; you cannot grasp it with your intellect and your five senses because they provide you with only part of the picture.

E very "ism," including perfection-ism, is a compulsive need to control that is generated by fear of painful emotions.

Perfectionism is looking outward in an attempt to soothe painful experiences by rearranging the external world, instead of looking inward to locate the sources of your pain and heal them.

Perfectionism is an enforced rigidity that prevents the natural flow of energy and intelligence. It is the continual judgment of yourself and others as deficient.

Perfectionism and anxiety go together.

Perfectionism is a perpetual flight into an illusory future that cannot be attained.

Emotional awareness is relaxing into the present moment, even when that moment contains painful emotions.

The desire to please other people is a potent way to distract yourself from what you are feeling.

The impulse to please other people is a powerful dynamic that is generated by fear of loss.

The need to please covers extreme pain.

The desire to please is an attempt to change others in order to make the one who pleases feel better. Anger and the need to please are both generated by fear of extremely painful emotions.

Individuals who attempt to please and individuals who become angry both have authority issues.

Individuals who need to please and individuals who dominate through anger and rage always find each other. They are colleagues in the Earth school who are enrolled in the same class.

The challenge is to develop the courage to confront the pain that lies beneath the intense desire to please others.

Healing the need to please is a sacred task.

An authentically empowered personality is an individual who naturally creates harmony, cooperation, and reverence for Life.

The intention to become what you think another person wants you to be disrupts harmony, even though it may temporarily reduce tension.

An individual who needs to please will try to gauge how others are feeling and how to make them happy so that he or she—the one who pleases—will feel safer.

An individual who needs to please is always tense.

One who attempts to please places his or her sense of self-worth completely in the hands of others.

When attempts to please fail, resentment emerges. The one who needs to please then steps onto the other side of the dynamic and strives to manipulate through anger.

Pleasing prevents you from experiencing your emotions because you are trying to feel the emotions other people are experiencing. You become lost in the attempt.

Attempting to please others narrows your emotional experience to fear and anxiety, with moments of relief when you feel you have succeeded.

S ince no one can please other people all the time, those who try engage in a fruitless effort that continually takes them away from their feelings.

The goal of pleasing others is to avoid experiencing emotions that are too painful or shameful to confront. Pleasing others is a technique to isolate you from your fear of losing love.

The strategy of pleasing others does not appear as a strategy to those who use it. It appears to be the only way their lives can be. They cannot imagine other ways of being.

Vacating is daydreaming, absent-mindedness, and the inability to focus on the task at hand. Vacating is an escape from the inner work you need to do.

Your soul is interested in how you use your energy—what you create—and whether you achieve your greatest potential. It sees the experiences of your life as part of a larger, richer, more complete picture than the one you can see.

Accomplishing the work that you were born to do is fulfilling, satisfying, and blissful. It ignites your creativity.

Vacating is a way of keeping yourself from all that will bring meaning, purpose, and fulfillment into your life. It is a choice to stay stuck rather than to work at changing.

When you vacate your awareness of the present moment, the present moment continues nonetheless. It has no end and no beginning, but your time on the Earth does.

You would neither fear nor forget the present moment if it were blissful. Authentic power is a blissful experience, not a painful one.

Recognizing moments in which your awareness lapses and mindless activities begin to fill your day is part of developing authentic power.

Vacating is never in response to a circumstance. It is a pattern of distancing yourself in order to avoid an awareness of what you are feeling.

Some people spend their lives without awareness of themselves as the central character in their own movie. The opportunities the Universe provides you to rewrite the script of your life never cease from the time you enter the Earth school until you leave it.

Your energy processing system is your real-time, personal, always available spiritual tutor.

The journey you are on is toward wholeness.

Boredom is a flight from what is important. Like workaholism and perfectionism, it is a way of distracting yourself from inner experiences.

B oredom is deep-rooted resistance to experiencing emotions after all efforts to distract attention from them have been ineffective.

The root of boredom is resistance to painful emotions.

You were not born to lose yourself in activities. Your purpose on Earth is to give the gifts your soul desires to give.

The parts of yourself that oppose the intentions of your soul—harmony, cooperation, sharing, and reverence for Life—are the parts that are frightened.

Boredom is your fuller life calling to you and your fear of hearing the call.

Perfectionists and workaholics ignore the present moment by focusing on activities and circumstances. Bored individuals ignore the present moment by pushing circumstances away.

A bored individual does not value his or her own life.

Boredom is weariness following the failure to find meaning externally, and the refusal to examine the meaning of that failure. For the bored individual, lethargy and weariness replace activity.

Workaholics and perfectionists pour their energy into external circumstances. Bored people pour their energy into avoiding them.

Boredom is a self-imposed numbness. It is a retreat into a shell, a disconnecting from others, from yourself, and from Life.

Boredom is the opposite of reverence. It is a demonstration of a
profound lack of respect for Life
in all its elements.

Idol worship is paying homage to, or being dominated by, an ideal. The idol most people worship is an internal image of who or what they think they should be.

The role an idol worshipper worships is the role he thinks he should play.

The function of idol worship is to avoid living your life directly and fully. Idol worship places a screen between you and your experiences. The idol worshipper ignores her inner signals, namely her emotions, and acts as she thinks her idol would act.

I f you use a role to create your sense of self-worth, you are an idol wor-shipper.

If an emotion does not fit the role an idol worshipper thinks he should play, he attempts to substitute an emotion he thinks he should feel.

At the heart of idol worship is a feeling of powerlessness.

Idol worship originates in fear, perpetuates fear, and expresses fear. It leads you away from empowerment, not toward it.

A Daredevil creates fears to overcome in order to avoid what is truly frightening. Though he has courage, all of his accomplishments divert his attention from what is terrifying, not merely frightening—his emotions.

A Daredevil does not have the courage to open himself or herself to love, so admiration is the mistaken substitute.

Every idol worshipper, including the Daredevil, is lonely and afraid to reach out in tenderness and openness. He is too frightened of the interactions that come with intimacy to attempt it.

An idol worshipper has no inner sense of value apart from the self-image he or she has created, and all of his or her efforts go into maintaining that image.

No idol worshipper—player of a role—relates honestly with himself or herself or with others. The longer the illusion of glamour—or goodness, innocence, shrewdness, or fearlessness—is maintained, the greater is the potential shock of looking at the consequences it has created.

A glorious life generates joy moment by moment. It requires the courage to face life's most difficult challenges—the pain of powerlessness, of feeling unloved and unlovable—and to change.

It is natural to be grateful for your life, and to look forward to each day.

An impenetrable optimist lives in the fantasy that all is for the best. Ironically, all *is* for the best; but an impenetrable optimist cannot truly know that because he refuses to experience his deeper emotions.

When impenetrable optimists can't get what they want, they believe that they don't really want it.

An impenetrable optimist uses optimism as a shield against painful emotions and presents an appearance of happy acceptance. This masks the pain of unmet expectations, fear of failure, and fear of rejection.

Impenetrable optimism is not the same as the optimism born of an individual's awareness of the compassion and wisdom in the Universe.

Your emotions tell you what your soul wants you to know.

False optimism is a blinder, but it cannot keep you from stumbling because of what you don't see.

You can pretend that all is for the best, but if you fear your fear, anger, jealousy, or vengefulness, you do not believe it.

When you welcome your emotions as teachers, every emotion brings good news, even the ones that are painful.

Entitlement is the belief that you have the right to what you desire, regardless of what others desire. It is a perception that you are fundamentally superior. Beneath entitlement is a very different reality.

Entitlement prevents intimacy.

Lack of intimacy creates isolation, and isolation leaves you feeling un-appreciated. You can't heal the pain of these feelings until you heal the need to feel entitled.

Entitlement requires the appearance of invulnerability. This hides a terror of rejection and ridicule. The more frightened you are, the more entitled you feel yourself to be.

Entitlement is temporary protection against the fear that the Universe is not big enough, or abundant enough, to meet your needs. It is. Your desires are always met when they are the same as the needs of your soul.

Alcohol and drug addiction are symptoms. The cause of both is intense emotional pain. When these underlying painful emotions are continually present and no effort is made to heal their causes, a dependence upon drugs and alcohol results.

Finding and healing the cause of emotional pain is at the core of spiritual growth.

Every painful emotion points to a part of the personality that does not share the elevated perceptions of the soul.

Healing an addiction requires an inward journey that demands courage, work, and commitment because it involves acknowledging and examining your greatest inadequacies.

Every moment of emotional pain is a place to start a journey only you can take.

The Universe nourishes you continually. When you close yourself to that nutrition, you feel the need to provide it for yourself. It is not calories you seek, but contact with your soul. No amount of chocolate, cookies, chips and salsa, or macaroni and cheese can substitute for that.

Y ou cannot receive too much nourishment from the Universe any more than you can breathe too much air.

Diet and exercise cannot reach the root of obsessive eating.

When you indulge your anger, jealousy, vengefulness, or any other form of fear, you turn your back on the nourishment the Universe provides you. Indulging in your emotions is like surrounding yourself with food and not eating. Feeling your emotions with the intention of learning from them is like eating from a banquet that never ends.

Emotional awareness is the first step in learning how to receive the nourishment the Universe provides for you.

When you eat to fill a hunger that food cannot satisfy, your body becomes larger than it needs to be. As you learn to receive the nourishment that the Universe provides, your body assumes a form that expresses its own balance.

The release of energy in love and trust produces health, contentment, gratitude, and joy.

A life on the Earth is the opportunity to create authentic power.

When your focus is on sex, your ability to experience your emotions is reduced or incapacitated.

Even the excitement and fear accompanying a potential sexual interaction are hidden behind a screen of fantasy that separates a sexual addict from the object of his or her attraction.

Addictive sexual attraction is a defense against awareness of the most painful experience in the Earth school—feeling powerless.

A sexual addict is an individual in acute pain, consumed by feelings of inadequacy.

The experience of addictive sexual attraction is a flag that signals a craving for meaning, purpose, and value.

A sexual addict goes from one person to another on a never-ending search for sexual satisfaction, hoping each time that the next partner will be his or her salvation.

The more intense the pain of fear, unworthiness, and feeling unlovable becomes, the more obsessive is the need of a sexual addict.

An addictive sexual attraction is never to another person. It is to an image you hold of that person. Addictive sexual interactions are barriers to intimacy, though they may appear to be intimate.

When emotional difficulties arise, other people become sexually attractive. This happens to marriage partners as well as to individuals who are not married. In loving sexual relationships, partners are not interchangeable.

Connecting the experience of addictive sexual attraction with the avoidance of painful emotions is a significant step in healing an addiction to sex.

It is impossible to have a sexual interaction without deepening the emotional connection between the partners.

Power struggles are artifacts of an earlier form of human evolution that is no longer constructive—pursuit of the ability to manipulate and control.

Every power struggle is an expression of the understanding of power as the ability to manipulate and control what appears to be external, including other people. This is the pursuit of external power.

The pursuit of external power without reverence is the cause of every conflict, cruelty, and painful emotion.

Reverence is an appreciation of Life in all its forms, the realization that there is nothing but Life.

The pursuit of power without reverence produces one thing—power struggles.

When the outcome is more important to you than the activity, you are in a power struggle.

The pursuit of external power is always an attempt to avoid pain.

Creating authentic power is using your will to change your life— finding the sources of your pain and changing them into sources of gratitude.

A power struggle collapses when you withdraw your energy from it. Power struggles become uninteresting to you when you change your intention from winning to learning about yourself.

Power struggles illuminate dynamics within you that you must change in order to create authentic power.

Savior searching is the effort to locate a person or a circumstance that can deliver you from discomfort.

Romantic attraction is the experience of locating a savior. He or she appears to have everything you need to complete your life. You feel this individual will solve your problems, eliminate your inner struggles, and bring you joy.

The power of a romantic attraction is the promise of permanent release from pain.

The collapse of a romantic attraction begins when you realize your savior cannot deliver, and your anxieties, fears, resentments, and self-doubts return. Then you begin the search for salvation all over again.

You place upon your saviors the responsibility for doing the work that only you can do. Every attempt to place your emotions in the hands of someone else is an attempt to escape from painful emotions.

The search for a savior brings a brief respite from your experience of painful dynamics, but it does not change them.

When you place as much attention on what you are feeling as you put on the search for a savior, you become your own salvation.

You are the source of your own happiness. Only your blessings can ease the pain in your heart.

Y ou do not need to be saved from your painful emotions any more than you need to be saved from the messenger who brings news that can change your life.

Judging others is a way of attempting to change the world, or reorder it to your own specifications.

You lose power to the people and circumstances you judge. They capture your attention in the same way that a movie does.

When you judge others, you forget who you are, what your goals and desires are, and, more importantly, what you are feeling.

When you judge, you see only what is objectionable to you—what makes you feel uncomfortable.

Indulging in a compulsion, including the compulsion to judge, is like taking pills to dull the pain. Stop taking them.

When you judge others, you judge yourself. If you did not possess the characteristics you so disdain, you would not have such an emotional reaction to them.

When you judge someone else, it is because you have recognized in that person characteristics you have not yet identified in yourself. Until you can acknowledge that those characteristics are parts of your personality, you will become enraged, angry, and disappointed when you see them in others.

Until you have felt your own pain, you cannot feel the pain of others.

Judging is a preemptive attack against that which you most desire—intimacy and acceptance—that is launched before you can be rejected or refused.

Your judgments of others, yourself, and the Universe will not stop until the pain that creates them is healed.

Stress is the consequence of resistance. When you resist circumstances in your life, you produce stress with that misplaced energy.

The amount of stress in your life is determined by how much energy you expend resisting your life.

S tress is your indication that you are resisting your experience in the present moment. It is the same as saying to a river, "You should not be flowing here, but there."

R elief from stress is freedom.

Accepting the present moment does not mean that you cannot change your life. On the contrary, it allows you to see clearly what needs to be changed. You cannot change your life without accepting it first.

Once you greet your life without resistance, you can determine what you need to change in order to create the circumstances and experiences that you desire.

Resisting an emotion prevents you from exploring it. The first step in changing the dynamic that creates an emotion is experiencing the emotion.

R esistance to your life is lack of trust in the Universe.

Authentic power is freedom from fear and awareness of your creative power as a soul. It is appreciation of the wisdom and compassion of the Universe.

An authentically empowered individual is a compassionate and patient friend with herself or himself. Creating that friendship begins with emotional awareness.